To the Six
Gang.
Thanks for your help.
This rocks!

Simon

May 2012.

First published in Great Britain by Project 44 Limited 2012

Copyright© Project 44 Limited

Simon Sear asserts the moral right to be identified as the author of this work.

ISBN 978-0-9571946-0-1

Printed in England

CONTENTS

INTRODUCTION

M any people are unhappy with their lives these days; whether it's their jobs, their home lives, their weight or just a sense of a lack of fulfilment and they would like to make some changes. Kencho is a transformational process, based on modern psychology and practical experience that will change your life and make you happier.

Personally, I find some psychology text books too complicated and academic and some of the self-help books too fluffy and decided to write a practical guide, full of exercises, that anyone can use to make changes to their life with the intention of becoming more balanced, happier, fulfilled and successful.

I wanted to create something easy to understand and follow like a modern diet or fitness plan, but for someone's personal wellbeing and mental health rather than weight loss. I truly believe that if you follow Kencho as laid out here it will change your life; I've done it myself.

I think I had a pretty average upbringing in deepest Essex, England: comprehensive school, three bedroom semi, nine GCSEs, three A levels, too many parties, Kylie Minogue and Jason Donavon, Guns and Roses, 7 inch singles, vinyl LPs with proper sleeves, Evel Knievel and Soda Stream.

Somehow after a year of work, once I'd left sixth form, I became the first person in my family to go to university. Actually it was a polytechnic; my grades weren't good enough for a proper university. My parents grew up in the East End of London and didn't even go to sixth form, let alone Uni. I was the first.

Anyhow, I was drawn to psychology and business studies and somehow managed to secure a degree in psychology. At the end of the course I had every intention of being a full time business psychologist and even went on to study a Master's Degree on day release in Occupational and Organisational psychology. However, fate dealt me another set of cards and I ended up working in change as a business analyst and project manager.

To cut a long story short, over the next 15 years or so (yes, I'm now 40 as I write Kencho!) I've published several books, progressed up the greasy pole of promotion to become a young IT Director at 2 multinational companies and eventually I've ended up as an independent consultant. For the last three years I've been plying my trade as a senior consultant through my own company; Project 44 Limited.

I have a beautiful, high achieving wife, three balanced and wonderful children, a nice house, a cool car, nice holidays, drink nice wine and go to some of the best restaurants.

I don't tell you this to boast, but to illustrate that a regular working class boy from Essex can obtain a high achieving life through having an evolving plan, commitment, a bias for action and a good understanding of themselves. Fundamentally, that's what Kencho is: It is my own personal transformational process combined with sound psychological research and tools.

I hope that you find it useful and I look forward to perhaps talking to you someday about your achievements.

I've found that knowing myself, having some kind of plan and taking action is one of the keys to success, fulfilment and making the right choices. What does your personality say about you? How will you design your life to be the most fulfilled and happiest you can be and will you take the actions needed to make it happen?

345

Kencho is based on a 345 formula; 3 Sources of Happiness, 4 Steps in the journey and 5 principles.

This is designed to help people easily remember it and understand how it fits together. There is a more detailed description of each number later, but let's take a look at what 345 means:

3 Sources of Happiness

Dr Martin Seligman, one of the pioneers of Positive Psychology, puts forward a framework that helps us think about how happiness works. Based on looking at the findings of research into happiness, unhappiness and motivation the framework has three elements at its core:

- Happiness from Pleasure

- Happiness from using our Strengths and Virtues (personality matching)

- Happiness from helping others

Happiness from pleasure relates to the good emotional feelings we get from enjoying experiences such as shopping, smoking, drinking, being in the limelight, going to the cinema or theatre, eating, taking drugs, having sex, etc.; The things that in our modern world that have become easily accessible. But somehow they often only last for a short period before we need more of them. Fundamentally the feeling of contentment we get from them is only temporary and it somehow just skims the surface.

For example, the more pleasure we obtain from an activity like drinking wine or beer the less positive the impact it has on us and the more we need to keep sustaining the shot of pleasure. There are diminishing returns from each extra unit of something we consume. The third drink never gives as much pleasure as the first; whether it's a beer, coca cola or wine.

On the other hand, happiness gained from doing activities that match our personality characteristics delivers a feeling of deep contentment when our lives and the activities we undertake make us feel like we're in the zone; in the flow of life. Activities that make us feel good and that click with us. An example might be a racing driver; they get a deep sense of fulfilment from driving at high speeds around a race track, but it is not a laugh a minute exercise. It requires concentration, skill, a natural ability and action. The sense of fulfilment is far deeper than pure pleasure. Within Kencho this is type of happiness is known as Personality Matching. Research shows that contentment from these activities is long lasting and reaches much deeper.

The final element of positive psychology involves doing something for other people. The evidence is overwhelming that when we do something for someone else we are left with a deep warm glow that lasts and lasts. This last type of happiness is big with Western Governments and media; probably in response to the questions on ethics and morality coming off the back of the financial crisis that has engulfed the Global economy and society over the last few years.

4 Steps in the Journey

Over the years I have worked with many individuals and organisations and I have had the opportunity to refine the Kencho transformation process into four steps; knowing yourself, clarifying your actions, planning and getting on with it!

Kencho involves following a series of steps that will take you through natural growth and transformation.

Step 1: Know Yourself

The initial Knowing Yourself step focuses on you becoming more aware of who you are; your personality characteristics, your strengths and your blockers. This is something that takes time and needs to involve talking to other people who can give you feedback and insights that you might not be able to see yourself.

Step 2: Clarify your Actions

After understanding yourself you will start to develop your own set of actions for the life you want to lead now and in the future. You will begin by visualising it, but quickly move into shaping specific and practical actions that you can realistically implement quickly and effectively.

Step 3: Plan Your Future

Many people are good at analyzing themselves and understanding who they are and intuitively know what their goals are and what they should do to change their lives but somehow they do not make it happen. The difference I have found between high achievers and those people who seem to drift through life is that high-achievers have some kind of plan and a bias to act.

During the final two steps of Kencho you will focus on setting yourself up for success by having a clear practical and deliverable plan.

Step 4: Get on with it!

During steps 2 and 3 people start to articulate where they want to go and how they are going to get there. This, to some extent, is an academic exercise; it is a theoretical piece of paper at this point. The last step then, is to get on with it; to start taking action.

This is often the stumbling block where people start to fall by the wayside. Often people get caught up in analysis paralysis. They get caught up in Steps 2 and 3 and spend ages polishing and refining their actions and plans. Individuals and organisations start to spin on the same point and do not make progress in transformation.

It is so important that in Step 4 you start taking action; making changes and realise you goals. In Kencho there are some tricks and exercises you can undertake to dramatically increase your chances of success including Twenty10.

5 Kencho Principles

Underlying the journey are 5 key principles that help shape the outcome:

Principle 1: Being happy is good for us and is locked into our genes.

Evidence shows that happy people are more resilient, live longer, are more innovative and work harder. What's not to like about being happy? Mother Nature designed us to seek happiness and fulfilment in order to survive as a species. It's survival of the fittest.

Principle 2: We are born with our personality and can do little to change it.

Long-term studies indicate that the majority of our personality is in our genes. There are triggers and events that can shape us in certain ways, but fundamentally, as anyone with kids will testify, we're born with our personality characteristics and changing them is hard to do. We are better to understand them and to focus our energy on designing our lives to get the best out of them.

Principle 3: We are happiest when our lives match our personalities.

The happiest people (and those that live the longest and are most productive) are those that have a lifestyle that matches their personality characteristics. We've all been in the 'zone' where time and energy just seems to be flowing. Contented people have more of those experiences every day.

Principle 4: Focusing on improving 'negative' personality traits doesn't work.

Accepting that we are born with our personality means we accept that we have both positive and negative characteristics. Any corporate employee who has to sit through the annual performance assessment cycle will testify that making fundamental changes to the way you are at work is extremely difficult. That's because it's part of your unconscious personality; you can't easily choose. What's more, it takes a huge amount of energy to do so and is a huge distraction from the positive aspects of who we are. We're therefore much better off focusing on enhancing our positives.

Principle 5: Dwelling on the past doesn't help us with the future.

Kencho isn't about years of counselling or psycho-analysis, it's about the here and now and the future. It's about creating practical interventions and plans you can undertake to make long lasting changes to your life with immediate positive results.

HOW TO USE THIS BOOK

B efore you start the Kencho process read through the whole book and exercises so you get a good idea of how it all fits together.

Like psychology in general, Kencho is an art rather than a science. It is a process for navigating transformational change rather than a prescriptive set of scientific or engineering laws. Somehow over the last hundred years with all of the positive and progressive advances in science we seem to have lost other aspects of what it is to be human. For one thing, in our everyday lives we seem to have lost the art of listening to our intuition which is where a lot of our unconscious personality or character lives.

Trust your Intuition and Start Taking Action.

Intuition is the communication tool of the unconscious mind and since our unconscious is where our deep rooted personality characteristics resides it is something we need to be in tune with in order to live a fulfilled and balanced life. Kencho is a different experience for everyone, but it is just that; an experience.

Take your Time

It's important that you undertake Kencho over a period of time. It involves undertaking exercises, sleeping on things, talking to other people and taking action. It is not a quick fix for solving specific issues, but a transformational process that will take you from where you are today to a much more fulfilled, contented and successful life.

The first intense steps in your journey will take you about 3 - 4 weeks to complete. After that you will undertake 20 day action plans over weeks and possibly months to implement the actions you identify. This is not a quick fix self-help book; it is a journey that will deeply transform your life to be more fulfilled and happier.

Write stuff down

I have designed this book to be your own personal journal of your transformation. It is your toolbox and journal where you can write and record all of the things that happen through the process. It's important that you write down all of the things that result from undertaking an exercise, having a conversation or simply something that pops into your head.

> Take your time. You can't transform your life in two hours, a long weekend or seven days.

There is plenty of writing paper in the journal and once you start writing you will want to come back to your notes over and over. So it's important that you can read your own writing and be clear about what it was that you meant when you wrote it. You'll be surprised the amount of information that starts to come from your unconscious mind that you will readily forget if you don't write it down.

Create a Kencho Club

If you are interested in working with others why not create a local Kencho Club. It is part of being human that we are social animals. We often get inspiration from other people, from other's actions and stories. We also have a natural tendency to help each other and think things through by discussing them with other people.

Creating your own club of likeminded people can be hugely rewarding for all and it's free. Decide on a venue; maybe take turns to host an evening or meet in the pub or local restaurant. There are no rules to creating a club; meet where you want and however often.

Some ideas for creating your club include:

- Create a Facebook page
- Link to others of Facebook
- Hold regular weekly meetings at the same time and venue
- Elect an 'organiser' to co-ordinate the group
- Create 121 meetings if you need to
- Have people come and talk to the group

Find a Buddy or Coach

Being social animals we often learn the most from talking to other people. During your transformation journey you are going to need to get another opinion from time to time. You will need to work with someone you trust and respect who can listen and play back some of your thoughts. They must be honest and a good communicator.

It is up to you how often and when you meet up and talk to them. I make some suggestions during the book; whether it's face to face, on the phone or on Skype, but it is really up to you.

Tweet or Facebook your journey

One of the benefits of having a buddy, a coach or belonging to a Kencho club is that your public commitment to change will help motivate you to take action. Another technique is to tweet or Facebook your goals and your progress.

You can tweet your own personal journey or find other people online going through the same transformational process. You are more likely to succeed if you do it publicly.

Use it with www.kencho.org

Your Kencho book has been designed to fit seamlessly with the online website. On it you will find some videos to help you, some up to date exercises and materials to support you through it; like guidelines for completing questionnaires. You do not have to use the website, it is completely up to you, however, you will find updates, links and other useful material.

Get Social

Whether we are introverts or extroverts we all need a network in which to act. Having a rich social network to talk to and reflect with is one of the keys to being fulfilled and more content with our lives.

As you go through the Kencho process you will need to reflect and talk through your experience with other people. It's important that as you undertake your transformational journey you listen to other people and bounce around some of the thoughts, ideas and feelings you are having.

Make sure the people you involve are 'good for you' and have a positive outlook. In your heart you know who you can trust and who you can't. Make sure you are clear with yourself that those people who are negative and likely to sabotage your thoughts are kept at arm's length.

3 SOURCES OF HAPPINESS

P reviously, I outlined the three sources of happiness that are at the heart
of Kencho:

- Happiness from Pleasure

- Happiness from Personality Matching

- Happiness from Helping others

Being happy is not just some wholesome idea, but a genetic disposition
that is in our genes. In the next section, I explain why it is so important to
humans to be happy and why it is the core Principle in Kencho, but before
that, just a few more notes on happiness.

We each have a different natural level of happiness and fulfilment.

Living a happy and contented life isn't about being the life and soul of
the party; the upbeat, popular centre of attention with a carefree take on
life. It's about living in balance with your own happiness level. Research
suggests that each of us has a balance of happiness that we are born with
and naturally level off at. We all know friends or have acquaintances that
are annoyingly happy. They are the ones full of energy, bouncing around,
telling jokes, making people laugh; the ones who my kids love and want to
spend time with. The blokes who make me feel a little bit rubbish about my
sometimes serious character. I could never be that outwardly jolly for that
length of time; it's impossible.

Research shows us that these people have an innate high level of happiness. Their balance and tide mark is higher than the average person; they were born that happy go lucky way. Equally, there are another group of people we all know who seem to be serious and generally low in happiness; the sceptical ones who don't seem to laugh out loud, they just seem to raise the odd smile. These people may feel perfectly happy with their lives and themselves without needing to be the life and soul of the party. Their happiness (the outward emotion and expression of it) is set at a much lower level than the average and is polls apart from Mr Jolly. Again, they were born that way.

My friend Mr Jolly; The annoying one!

The majority of people are born in the mid-range of happiness. Our balance is genetically set to a point that is good for us and good for the longevity of our genes.

Living our lives in such a way that we are in balance with our unique level of happiness will ensure we live the most contented life we can. It's attractive to think we can all be Mr Jolly; but the evidence suggests we can only move our own balance up to a new point in small steps.

However, the good news is that if we live at our balance point, negative events will only temporarily impact our level and we will move back to the balance point in a short space of time. Research shows that losing your job or getting divorced will only have a temporary impact. The only experiences that really seem to have a lasting negative impact relate to trauma. A time when something traumatic happens that we weren't expecting. If a partner has a long term illness which eventually leads to an untimely death we have had time to get used to the idea and our unhappiness at the event is temporary. After four months or so our balance will return to its average range. If, however, our partner is killed in a tragic accident on the motorway or by a stranger in the street we never really recover to our previous balance. Such an event pushes our balance down to a lower level.

5 PRINCIPLES

A t the heart of Kencho are some fundamental principles that help to shape interventions, exercises and the tools used to help implement the change you are looking for during the 4 steps.

Principle 1: Being happy is good for us and is locked into our genes.

Bookshop shelves are full of self-help volumes promising to make us happier and enable us to live the life we should be living. They describe the habits of successful people, the secrets of meditation and ancient wisdoms. There are whole sections of books that have sold millions of copies worldwide in multiple languages.

For years I thought it was a nice aspiration but I didn't have a great sense that it meant much more than some fluffy good intentions. However, I recently found out about some interesting research; the results of which explain why we all seek out happiness: It's in our genes!

The research tells us that people find happy people more attractive. Look down the dating adverts online or in the newspaper and note how many ads mention GSH; Good Sense of Humour. We are pre-programmed to like happy people and dislike unhappy people. How many times have you experienced the black cloud that hangs over an unhappy person and wanted to avoid them? They can bring the whole room or team down with their negative attitude. On the contrary, happy people can lift the mood and bring an overall sense of wellbeing and contentment. People gravitate towards positive people and want to be around them.

So to ensure we procreate and find a partner it's a good idea to be happy; Mother Nature made it so. But there's more; happy people live longer. Research data shows that the people who are more content have longer lives. Not only are they enjoying themselves more than unhappy people but they also live longer. Suffering lower levels of cancer and fatal diseases like heart disease.

Fulfilled people are also more innovative and come up with more solutions and ideas. It makes sense when you think about it. Put a bunch of positive people together who are in a good mood and you have a recipe for great brain storming and innovation.

They are also more resilient to the stresses and strains that life throws at us. Sure they will get knocked off balance by bad news and unfortunate events, but they are much more likely to bounce back if they have a happy disposition and sense of overall contentment compared to an unhappy one.

In summary, evolution has encouraged human beings to develop into being happy because it is good for us and good for humankind in general. Happy, contented people live longer, are more able to cope with stress and change, will come up with innovative solutions and are more likely to find a suitable mate. Being happy isn't just about some fluffy good intention; it's about ensuring an individual and their gene pool survive and prosper.

Principle 2: We are born with our personality and can do little to change it.

The nature or nurture question has long been debated in psychology. How much of who we are is determined by our genes and how much is determined by our environment; our parent's behaviour, our schooling, the people we meet, the groups we join, etc.?

There were those who thought we were a blank canvas; ready to be moulded into wonderful utilitarian members of society. The old Jesuit saying states;

> Give me the boy until the age of seven; I will give you the man.

They thought those who ended up in trouble did so because of poor parenting and only if they could get them early enough we could straighten them out. Equally, they presumed they could build a wonderful righteous civilisation through education, punishment and strict values.

Of course, they were partly right; our environment does have an impact on who we are. We dress like our group, we learn habits and knowledge from others, we react to situations as society expects. But, unless we have had some deep trauma, the evidence suggests that our personality is largely determined by our genes. Study after study into the lives of twins shows that even those separated at birth end up with extraordinarily similar personality characteristics, jobs and lifestyles.

Anyone with children will tell you how different each one of them is, how individual but, at the same time, often how similar they are to their parents, grand-parents or siblings. All of my children have different personalities and will end up in different jobs when they are older. They had the characteristics of themselves since they were born really and over the years certain characteristics have come to the fore more than others.

Having said that, they are all very similar in many traits too; they are all artistic, they all have good emotional intelligence and communication skills. You might argue that since my wife and I are strong in these areas it is no surprise they are too. We must have encouraged and taught them to be so.

Purely by living with us they could have learnt to be artistic and confident communicators. I think you'd partly be right, but there is too much evidence from the field of genetics that shows that these events are merely triggers that ignite an underlying personality characteristic. My kids had to have the raw ingredients to be arty in the first place.

We have all worked with people who are driven, others who are sensitive, those who are artistic or amazing teachers. No amount of education and learning gave them those underlying characteristics. They were born with them; it was Mother Nature. Father Nurture, on the other hand, gave them the environment and the triggers to discover, improve and hone them, but the underlying was there, deep in the unconscious.

We might now say a better quote than the old Jesuit saying might be something like this:

> Give me the child for a couple of hours and we can work out the type of subjects and career objectives that might suit them best and give them the best chance of living a happy and fulfilling life and probably a very financially rewarding one too.

Principle 3: We are happiest when our lives match our personalities.

We are at our most fulfilled and happiest when we feel completely at home with ourselves. Whether it is at work, at school, at home, a club or sports event, when we are doing something that fits our personality we feel like we are in the zone. We enjoy the flow of life. Time passes without being noticed and even if it is stressful and hard work it leaves us with a sense of fulfilment and contentment.

> Work is more than an exchange for money.

By The Way: You can't change your life by positive thinking alone. It is not possible. We all have to make physical changes and take action.

Principle 4: Focusing on improving 'weak' personality traits doesn't work.

Over the years I have seen many people coached at work or put into development roles to iron out some of the weaknesses of their personality.

Whilst you can help people develop or alter their behaviours, wholesale personality change just doesn't happen. For example, you can coach an individual to be less direct, but you'll never remove that trait of 'directness'. Fundamentally, one of the characteristics of that person is that they are direct in the way they engage and communicate.

The first thing that should be considered is not how to remove the trait, but how to place that person in a position where they can play to it. Somewhere it can actually have a positive impact on the company. Perhaps in project management within a tough and assertive industry; an environment where they need to quickly cut through the noise and deliver. Not in sales, marketing or customer services!

I have seen so many examples of where people have ended up in the wrong role at work. The organisation, being conscientious and people focused, then spends vast amounts of time and money to try and help them develop new personality characteristics or remove unwanted ones. This is like trying to grow a new arm or removing one from a person.

Unless they have some serious anti-social behavioural problems the organisation is better off spending the time and the money to match the individual's personality to the right job or cut them free and support them in finding a job in a new company with the right job and the right culture. Ultimately, a happy employee, who is fulfilled and works in 'their zone' is vastly more productive than the employee an organisation has to support, coach and train to be fundamentally someone else.

The same is true for children. We all want our kids to be successful, but to be truly successful and fulfilled we need to teach them who they are and guide them towards a career and a life that will match their personality strengths.

Principle 5: Dwelling on the past doesn't help us with the future.

Freud is probably the most famous psychologist of all time. His theories and psycho-analysis have become engrained in our culture; from the ego to the Freudian slip, his influence is deep. However, he was wrong about some stuff. Fundamentally, raking up our past problems and reliving them isn't actually a good way to make positive changes to your life. It doesn't set you free, it just reminds you how bad it was and replays it again in your mind. It can actually prolong the unhappiness and trap someone in a negative cycle. How many people get stuck in psycho-analytical therapy for years and years?

Do you 'Fight or Flight'?

When we experience a challenge we naturally become aroused and experience an emotional state of 'fight or flight.' We either naturally turn on our heels and flee or we rise to the challenge; pretty useful when faced with a predatory animal or attacking tribe.

Faced with the challenges of modern life, we still continue to experience the same emotional states. Some people seek to wind back the clock and live a simpler way of life, away from the stresses and strains of modern life; the Internet, Facebook, consumerism, bankers, capitalism, computer games, electronic banking, etc. Other people embrace the challenges and rise to them, adapt and change.

I believe that the only way we can prosper is by being progressive and grow as individuals. I believe that is something that truly makes us stand out from other animals; we have the capacity and the almost need to evolve, adapt and change. Fundamentally, Kencho works in harmony with this natural process.

4 STEPS IN THE JOURNEY

The remainder of your Kencho book takes you through the 4 steps in the journey. I have included a number of exercises for each step; designed to challenge you and to get you to move forward.

STEP 1: KNOW YOURSELF

Purpose: To discover the real you and build a solid base for the rest of the process

Duration: Two weeks

The first step to transforming your life; to make positive changes, is to understand yourself and where you are now. The reason this is important is because in order to become more fulfilled and in tune with your life you need to match your actions with your personality characteristics.

It is really important that you spend time on this initial first step. You'll probably want to start defining your actions and plan for transforming your life. That's a natural tendency that most of us have. However, you must resist this and spend some time actually understanding yourself.

This will involve some personal reflection and analysis, but also a lot of reflection and discussion with other people in your life. It's not something that can be rushed and I'll tell you why. Kencho is fundamentally about tuning in to your unconscious and, as such, during this step you will need to trust your own intuition and sometimes let things process behind the scenes for a while.

Our unconscious mind works in the background and often you will find that once you start Kencho things will come into your head at random times. This is just your unconscious mind doing its thing. When this happens write down what you feel and 'think' in your Kencho journal. Rushing this step will therefore leave you incomplete and will mean that later steps aren't as successful as they need to be for you to really transform your life. We have all had those moments when we have woken up in the middle of the night or suddenly remembered something we could not recall from the day before. That is your unconscious mind working away in the background.

In this section of your journal you will find lots of exercises designed to get to the heart of who you are. If you want to go online or use some self-help books to find other tools that is fine. The point is to keep the objective in mind:

> ## Discover the real you and build a solid base for your transformational journey.

We also focus on who you pretend to be; to yourself and to others. You will look at how your own and other people's expectations are shaping and blocking you from being happier and more fulfilled. This is much harder than it seems. We often spend more time thinking about other people than we spend thinking and reflecting on ourselves. When was the last time you asked someone for feedback?

The reason I keep it to 2 weeks is because less than a week is not long enough for your unconscious mind to process the information you receive whilst anything longer than two weeks does not add a whole lot of additional value. Action at this point (by moving to the next step), once you have got 80%, is much more productive than trying to find the remaining twenty percent.

During this step of the process you will probably start to think about some of the actions you want to take. That is perfectly natural and normal, but you should try to refrain from jumping past step 1 and straight to shaping actions as it will lead to a weaker transformation process.

Before you complete the following exercises in your journal, you need to feel relaxed, safe and curious. Let your mind be curious, not fearful, not looking for perfection or for anything in particular.

Identifying your Pleasures

As I said in an earlier part of your book, we do get happiness and fulfilment from experiencing pleasures and, although at the heart of Kencho is the principle that deep rooted fulfilment comes from living your life in tune with your personality characteristics it is still important to consider the activities you enjoy that give you pleasure.

Personally, I like drinking whisky and wine, going out to dinner with my wife and friends, going to the theatre, watching films, spending time with my kids, going to the gym, driving fast cars, reading books, being married, being a dad, being a leader, etc.

Some are pure pleasures, like drinking whisky or wine, whilst others, like being a dad or being married are major lifestyle choices. It's not worth getting caught up on the difference; just focus on the intent; which is to identify the things and experiences that give you pleasure. It's worth noting that pleasure from experiences will be much stronger than pleasure from having things.

It's important that you are clear on the things you like doing and the things that give you pleasure, because when you come to think about your own actions to achieve greater happiness you will want to do more of these things in your life. Designing your life to do more pleasurable activities is one of the key practical things you can do easily.

It won't have the same deep impact as designing your life to match your personality, but doing more of them will make you happier.

Exercise 1: Write down the things that give you pleasure

In the table below write down the things that give you pleasure and make you happy. Score them in this way:

1. Makes you happy when you are doing it, but leaves you with a feeling of regret afterwards

2. Makes you happy for the time that you are doing it

3. Makes you happy for short period of time afterwards

4. Makes you feel generally happy and fulfilled when you think about this pleasure

5. Gives you a deep sense of wellbeing and lasting happiness

The idea is to try and identify the things that give you short term pleasure and those that give you a longer lasting feeling of fulfilment.

PLEASURE	SCORE				
	1	2	3	4	5
	1	2	3	4	5
	1	2	3	4	5
	1	2	3	4	5
	1	2	3	4	5
	1	2	3	4	5
	1	2	3	4	5
	1	2	3	4	5

Now you have completed this, write a few notes on those things you should do more of. Think about; what is stopping you doing them?

Exercise 2: Write down the things that make you miserable

In the table below write down the things that make you miserable and unhappy. Score them in this way:

1. Makes you a bit miserable when you are experiencing it, but the feeling leaves you afterwards

2. Makes you unhappy for a short period of time after the actual experience itself

3. Makes you feel miserable and apprehensive thinking about it and doing it

4. Makes you feel generally unhappy when you think about this experience and you try and avoid it

5. The thought of it just makes you feel depressed; it fills you with dread.

The idea is to try and identify the things in your life that make you feel miserable so that in later stages you can plan out how to stop doing them and take action to remove them from your life where possible.

THING THAT MAKES YOU MISERABLE	SCORE				
	1	2	3	4	5
	1	2	3	4	5
	1	2	3	4	5
	1	2	3	4	5
	1	2	3	4	5
	1	2	3	4	5

Now you have completed this, write a few notes on why these things make you miserable and what you can do to avoid them or take them out of your life.

Personality Matching

In order to makes changes to your life you must first understand your personality and your current experiences. I have been working with people in change for a long time and this stage of Kencho is crucial to realising your goals. Whether it is personal changes to your lifestyle or a whole company, being clear on where you are now is fundamental.

> Follow your heart and your intuition. They know what you truly want to become.

Kencho is based on the principle that our unconscious, our intuition, our soul, whatever we call it, knows what makes us happy. We are all different, born with different personalities; different skills, desires, likes and wants. Understanding these and living our life in tune with them is one of the keys to happiness and fulfilment.

The exercises in this section will help you understand your own self to a much greater depth than you have before. It might be an emotional journey, but stick with it and you will be pleased with the results.

Exercise 3: Go online and complete a personality questionnaire

The objective of this exercise is to get to know you a little better through using an online tool. There isn't enough room in this book to include a whole personality test. You can find many of these online, like Myers Briggs, which have been around for a long while and will give you instant results. Usually you answer a number of random questions which are designed to provide you with a summary of your personality characteristics.

Do not rush this exercise. Give yourself plenty of time and space to complete it.

Step 1: Take an online personality questionnaire

You can take more than one if you want; it's entirely up to you, but there are diminishing returns after your take the first one.

They are often free to use online and require no technical competence, although you can also find some that are fee based. Personally, I'd just use a good Myers Briggs based questionnaire from a quality website; it's going to be good enough.

Check out Kencho.org for some good links.

Step 2: Note down the main characteristics

Once you have completed it, write down here the main characteristics of your personality and any weaknesses noted. For example, my profile comes up with personality characteristics like; project orientated, warm and genuinely interested in people, great people skills, service orientated, cooperative, well developed communication skills, etc. Some of the weaknesses include; resists being controlled, dislikes performing routine tasks and needs approval and appreciation.

Step 3: Discuss the results with someone else

Now sit down with your buddy, coach or someone you trust and talk through the results.

The intention of this conversation is to come away with a clear and succinct view of your key personality characteristics. In the space below I want you to summarise the main things you have found, it's worth having a read before you meet your buddy and write some notes based on the output of your personality test.

Step 4: List your Top 6 Strengths – remember these are personality characteristics.

Here are some examples:

- Coming up with new and innovative ideas to challenges and problems.

- Finishing things off and making sure all loose ends are tied up.

- Motivating other people comes easily to me. People like working with me.

Step 5: List your Top 3 Weaknesses – the things you are not good at and don't enjoy.

Here are some examples:

- Finishing things off; I always start new things and leave things half finished.

- Coming up with new ideas – I'm not particularly creative and prefer other people to come up with ideas that I implement.

It is ok to have weaknesses, we all have them. If they are practical skills we can often improve them, if they are personality based then we can design our goals and life to minimise using them. There is not point doing things you are not good at or do not enjoy over and over again. If we understand them and acknowledge them then we can manage them. Ignoring them just avoids dealing with them.

As I mentioned above, one of my weaknesses is that I dislike being controlled and doing routine tasks. That's why I took the choice to leave a successful corporate career and become an independent consultant and entrepreneur; being told what to do, a cog in the wheel and doing the same job day after day made me deeply unhappy. It took me a while to figure that out, but once I did it was one of the best decisions I ever made for my sense of wellbeing and fulfilment.

Step 6: Reflect on the whole exercise

Finally, I'd like you to reflect on this exercise and list 3 New Things you learnt about yourself – either from the test or from your conversation.

Wait 24 hours before you undertake any further exercises. It is important that this one sinks in.

Exercise 4: Create your own questionnaire for 5 people

This is something that can be quite daunting. Sometimes we are apprehensive about hearing feedback from other people for fear of not liking it. However, it is a very powerful and quick way to get an insight into yourself in a way that you might not have had before.

To make it the most effective it can be it is best to make it anonymous; the reason being that people feel less afraid to tell the truth. You will also feel like it is less personal too.

You should undertake this exercise after you have completed your personality questionnaire because you will have a much better understanding of the questions you want to ask. If you have a Buddy or a coach then you can also work with them on this exercise as it will give you further depth.

Step 1: Read your personality output

Make sure you have it fresh in your mind before you start to brainstorm the questions. Think about the personality strengths and development areas or weaknesses you identified.

Step 2: Brainstorm the questions you want to ask

Do not feel restricted at this point. Just write down all of the types of questions you think are important to understand a little more. I've listed below some sample questions to get you started:

- What things do I do well?
- What things do you think I enjoy the most?
- What job do you think I would be good at?

- What areas of development do you think I have?

- How could I help other people more?

You do not need to ask too many questions. Limit it to 6 although less is ok. It is more about the quality of the information you want to get back rather than the quantity.

Step 3: Pick your candidates carefully

You want positive and honest feedback from the people you ask, but you do not want negative or destructive feedback. Do not ask questions like 'What do you hate about me?' and do not ask for feedback from people you know might be overly negative or even spiteful. Trust your intuition on this one.

You want useful and constructive information that you can use to understand yourself in more depth. Examples might include, work colleagues, a parent, a best friend, one of your kids or your partner.

Step 4: Send out your questionnaire to 5 people

Talk to the people you are asking to complete it for you. Tell them about Kencho and what you are doing and ask for their help in giving you feedback. You will find some guidelines on the Kencho website for completing feedback for other people. Point them in that direction if they would like to know more.

Make sure you set a date for them to return the questionnaire to you. A few days are about right. (If it is anonymous have them email your buddy or coach).

Step 5: Summarise the feedback

In the following pages of your book write down the questions you asked and the main feedback points you got.

Step 6: Discuss the feedback

To make sense of the feedback it is important that you get someone else's perspective on it. If you have a Buddy or Coach then sit down with them and talk through the findings from your personal questionnaire. If not, then talk to someone you trust.

Step 7: Reflect

Finally, once you have read the feedback, discussed it and digested it then write a few final thoughts about what you learnt. Did you learn anything new? Did the exercise just reinforce what you already knew? How did you feel during the exercise? Would you do it again?

Exercise 5: Who do you pretend to be?

Many people wear different masks at different times, depending on who they are with; their partners, their friends, children, work colleagues, etc. Sometimes we need to do this, at other times we are restricting ourselves by not being true to ourselves and our underlying personality characteristics. Pretending to be something we are not drains a huge amount of energy and can be a huge distraction from living a fulfilled life.

During this exercise I want you to be honest with yourself and clarify who you pretend to be and where that is not aligned to what you have found out in the earlier exercises; your online personality test and your own personality questionnaire you gave out to other people.

Undertaking non-authentic behaviour is not a bad thing, by the way. It is often a defence mechanism to fit in or cope with a situation or it is where we find ourselves in a situation that is not in tune with our true selves and we therefore end up making up for a lack of natural flow by pretending to be something else. It does not make us bad people. It is a natural human response. The key however to living a more fulfilled life is to reduce the non-authentic and focus on matching our personality strengths with our life.

During this exercise we are trying to identify the non-authentic so that we can plan to remove them and focus more of our energy on to the ones we really do enjoy that make us feel good.

Step 1: Select 2 Life Scenarios where you experience non-authentic behaviour

I want you to take 2 scenarios from the list below (or others if you have significant others) and complete the tasks outlined for each. Trust your intuition and be honest with yourself. Only you really know the true and deep answers, although people you act with will also have many insights so if you feel brave enough to ask them, then do so.

Example Scenarios include:

- Who do you pretend to be at work?
- Who do you pretend to be with your partner?
- Who do you pretend to be with your parents?
- Who do you pretend to be with your children?
- Who do you pretend to be with a club or community you belong to?

Step 2: Complete 2 Scenarios in your book

Some people find that when they come to think about who they pretend to be they repeat many of their personality weak points or things that make them miserable. They become aware that they are covering over things they neither enjoy nor are they particularly good at. If that happens to you then this is very insightful and useful.

It means you have clarified areas in your life to change, that will, if removed lead to an increase in your overall level of fulfilment and happiness.

Scenario 1:

Given what you now know about yourself from the online personality questionnaire and what other people have fed back to you:

What behaviours do you exhibit in this scenario that are authentic?

_____

_____

_____

_____

_____

What behaviours do you exhibit that are non-authentic, those that you pretend?

_____

_____

_____

_____

_____

For these pretend behaviours, why do you undertake them?

_____

_____

_____

_____

_____

For these pretend behaviours, if you were to stop doing them, what would happen?

_____

_____

_____

_____

_____

Scenario 2:

Given what you now know about yourself from the online personality questionnaire and what other people have fed back to you:

What behaviours do you exhibit in this scenario that are authentic?

_____

_____

_____

_____

_____

What behaviours do you exhibit that are non-authentic, those that you pretend?

_____

_____

_____

_____

_____

For these pretend behaviours, why do you undertake them?

_____

_____

_____

_____

For these pretend behaviours, if you were to stop doing them, what would happen?

_____

_____

_____

_____

_____

Step 3: Who do you pretend to be?

After you have completed making notes for both scenarios, then summarise below the 3 most used behaviours you undertake that are not authentic to who you are; behaviours that are non-authentic and that you want to stop doing.

Exercise 6: Are you in the right job?

Going to work takes up a huge amount of our time, energy and focus. Getting it right and doing something you love is fundamental to living a fulfilled and happy life. If you are in a job now, then you may want to make changes to your current role or change direction entirely; we will get to that later. If you are at school and thinking about what you want to do, then this can be an equally as powerful exercise for you.

Step 1: Re-read the results from your previous exercises

Before you write anything re-read your personality characteristics.

Step 2: Ask the Million Dollar question!

During this exercise I want you to ask yourself one very simple question:

> If you got paid the same amount of money as you get today but could do any other job tomorrow what would it be?

Step 3: Write down your answers

Write down here what you answers are. You want to end up with a list of reasons you would like to do it. Make sure you are clear about the reasons you would like to have that job.

As you undertake this exercise, never start to think about money or income. Stick to type and characteristics of the job.

Step 4: What is stopping you 'really'?

Money might be a constraint, but there are always ways to solve problems, put that aside and identify what is 'really' stopping you; your parents; your loss of status, lack of motivation, fear of failing?

Think about it, discuss it with people you trust and make some notes. If you say money is the only blocker then I don't believe you.

Exercise 7: Do you Love your Love life?

If you have a significant partner in your life, then this is a great exercise that will have a short and long term positive impact on your relationship. If you do not have a partner you can adapt it to think about one of your parents or children.

This exercise takes a few days to complete, but can be done at the same time as other exercises in this step.

Day 1: Write down your feelings about a romantic partner in the form of a letter or short essay.

Day 2: Read what you wrote on Day 1 and list 10 things you love about that person.

Day 3: Re-read Day 1 and Day 2 and buy the person you are thinking about a card or write them an email or letter. Write a short note and include all the things you love about them.

Day 4: Make any final small changes to what you have written on Day 3 and then give them the email or the card.

Finally, write here how you felt when you gave them the letter, card or email and what their reaction was.

Exercise 8: Thank Someone

Our lives are so busy these days and so fast paced that sometimes we forget to be thankful for the things we do have and the people we have in our lives. Gratitude is a powerful human activity that we don't do often enough. Sure we say please and thank-you to strangers and drum it into our children that it is good manners, but how often do we really take the time to properly thank someone.

This is an extremely powerful and positive exercise and, although you might feel embarrassed by undertaking it, you should really try and overcome your fears and complete it. It is best completed face to face as I've laid out below, but if you are really that embarrassed you can write them a letter or email instead. Although this has a lower impact.

This exercise might take some time to complete, but it is really worth it; it often has a powerful effect on people undertaking change and on those that they interact with.

The reason for doing this exercise during Step 1: Knowing Yourself, is because it is an experience that will spark your unconscious into thinking more and more about the positive events that have happened in your life.

The aim is to prepare a short letter that you are going to read to someone you want to thank. It can be anyone; your parents, your friend, a teacher, one of your kids, anyone who you genuinely want to thank for something.

Step 1: Decide who you are going to thank.

Step 2: Write some notes in the space of a few days here in your book.

Step 3: Prepare your letter

From your notes in step 2, pull together a brief letter for the person you are thanking.

Step 4: Meet with the person and read to them what you have written. Make sure you deliver it nice and slowly and look at them as you say the words.

Step 5: Talk with the person about the contents of your letter.

Step 6: Write down how you felt during and after the meeting in the space below.

Exercise 9: Do something for 3 other people

This exercise will help you to understand how you feel when you do things for other people and to clarify what kind of actions make you feel good. Doing things for other people leads to deep rooted happiness and fulfilment and so it is important to start to tap into that early on in the Kencho process and to start to understand how it affects you personally.

Step 1: Undertake an action for someone else that is helpful. Don't buy someone something. Make sure it is an action that you have to complete.

They need not be huge gestures, they might, for example include picking a friend's kids up from school, making someone dinner from raw ingredients, booking tickets for a surprise trip to the movies, cleaning up, offering to fix something that has been broken for a while….. you get the idea.

Step 2: Once you have undertaken it ask yourself these questions and write the answer in your journal below:

What did you do?

_____

_____

_____

_____

_____

How did you feel when you were doing it?

_____

_____

_____

_____

_____

How did you feel a few days afterwards?

_____

_____

_____

_____

_____

What other things would you like to do in the future for other people that would give you a good feeling?

_____

_____

_____

_____

_____

Step 3: Repeat steps 1 and 2 for two other people.

Person 2

What did you do?

_____

_____

_____

_____

_____

How did you feel when you were doing it?

_____

_____

_____

_____

How did you feel a few days afterwards?

_____

_____

_____

_____

What other things would you like to do in the future for other people that would give you a good feeling?

_____

_____

_____

_____

_____

Person 3

What did you do?

_____

_____

_____

_____

How did you feel when you were doing it?

_____

_____

_____

_____

How did you feel a few days afterwards?

_____

_____

_____

_____

_____

What other things would you like to do in the future for other people that would give you a good feeling?

_____

_____

_____

_____

_____

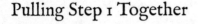

Pulling Step 1 Together

Over the last few weeks you have undertaken the Step 1 exercises in your book. Before you move on to Step 2 it is important to bring all of the information and things you have learnt together in order to have a good summary and base on which to build the next steps.

You need to summarise and make sense of the things you clarified and learnt. It is also important that you share this with at least one other person. If you have a buddy or coach helping you through this process then sit down with them and go over your summary; adding any notes or changes that come out of the conversation.

During Step 2 of Kencho you will read this summary before you undertake each exercise, so you need to make sure it is comprehensive, but not so long that you forget the beginning before you get to the end.

On the following pages answer the key 10 questions from this first step of Kencho.

What things give me the most pleasure?

_____

_____

_____

_____

_____

What things make me miserable?

_____

_____

_____

_____

_____

What are my 6 key personality strengths?

_____

_____

_____

_____

_____

What are my 3 personality weak areas (things I do not like doing or are not good at)?

_____

_____

_____

_____

_____

Who do I pretend to be, which I want to stop?

_____

_____

_____

_____

_____

What are the key messages other people gave me?

_____

_____

_____

_____

_____

Am I in the right job? (why or why not?)

_____

_____

_____

_____

_____

Who am I grateful for in my life? (why?)

_____

_____

_____

_____

_____

How did I feel when I did things for other people?

_____

_____

_____

_____

_____

What have I got from Kencho step 1?

_____

_____

_____

_____

_____

STEP 2: CLARIFY YOUR ACTIONS

Purpose: To be clear on the things you want to change and achieve
Duration: 1 - 2 weeks

Now that you have a better idea of who you are it is time to start to visualise the type of future that you want to achieve and the changes and actions you are going to undertake in order to realise your future. Some people will want to change their lifestyle, lose weight, find a new job, start going to the gym, take up a new hobby, etc.

> Some of the most profound personal changes are the small ones that each of us can make every day.

Before we start to identify your goals, let's remind ourselves why we want to make changes. You will have your own reasons, but I find it really useful to remind people of the evidence of why is makes sense to be happier, more fulfilled and more content:

- You live longer
- You are more resilient to the stresses and strains of life
- You will be healthier
- People will find you more attractive
- You will be more innovative and have more ideas

During this phase it is important to keep your mind open and try to not think about how or when you will make the changes.

The first thing to do is read back what you have written about yourself.

Have the summary you wrote for Step 1 each time you undertake an exercise in Step 2 fresh in your mind. It's important you do this as it brings you back to the results of the hard work you have put in to date.

When you clarify your actions bear in mind why you want to achieve them and the benefits you will see as a result.

Happiness from pleasure

Many self-help books take a spiritual approach to transformation and change. Espousing a more spiritual and slightly fluffy view if I'm honest, and, whilst this suits many people, my experience is that it also puts a lot of people off. Partly, I think, because people actually like many things that aren't potentially good for them. For example, many people like drinking alcohol, eating chocolate, going shopping, buying art and smoking, even when they know some are bad for them.

These things give many people a great sense of pleasure and rather than try to preach that they should learn not to, Kencho is about acknowledging you get a sense of happiness from pleasures and should make them part of your life. You need to make sure you do them in balance, but, at the end of the day, the risk-reward payoff is only something you have to feel comfortable with.

If it makes you feel good then why not enjoy it? If it makes you fat, tired, at risk of lung cancer, etc. then stop doing it or cut down. Only you can truly decide and have control.

Fulfilment from personality matching

Matching the design of our lives with our underlying personality characteristics is key to living a fulfilled and contented life and is at the heart of Kencho. Whether it is the job we do, the course we study, the friends we have or the hobbies we undertake, the way we live our life determines our mental health.

> We've lost sight of the importance of Character on the life we lead; the jobs we do, the parents we are, the hobbies we enjoy.

Today we live in a busy and fast paced society, where, at least in the developed world, we have instant gratification, running water, heating, electricity, food, social care, etc. The continual progression and inventiveness of human kind has made life pretty convenient. Imagine then a human society only a short period ago where life was a lot less convenient and tougher. It was like that for thousands of years and Mother Nature designed us to be fulfilled and content when we experienced a series of activities in our daily lives and these are still true today.

Deep happiness, or rather fulfilment, is not only about having more and more pleasurable acts; it is far more complicated than that. It is also about undertaking activities or experiences that make us feel content deep down inside our unconscious. Research has shown these to be:

- Challenging Activities that require skill and learned knowledge and/or experience

- An activity that requires dedicated concentration

- We are in control of the activity

- We are clear on the goals of the activity

- We become so engrossed in the activity we become 'at one' with it

- We get into the zone, and time seems to fade away

Remember the example I gave earlier about the racing driver? All of the above apply.

Fulfilment from helping others

The third area that will improve your unconscious level of contentment and make your happier is doing something for someone else.

We all get a nice warm feeling from doing something for others. However, we get the best shot of happiness when we do something for someone when it is one of our personality character strengths. For example, I get some of the best fulfilment from helping other people think about things in a different way. I am good at thinking about problems and solutions in a creative and innovative way. I'm also quite direct so I get a deep sense of fulfilment from challenging other people to think about new ways to think about problems and come up with creative solutions. They don't even have to pay me. I'll gladly do it for free. It makes me feel good!

During this second step you will undertake a series of exercises that will help you clarify practical actions you can take to ensure you experience happiness from all three sources.

Exercise 10: Imagine Your Funeral

Imagine that you are very old and, in fact, you have just died. Imagine it is your funeral and a close friend is standing in front of a large crowd of well-wishers who have come to pay their last respects to you. Your friend is about to read out your own eulogy.

In the space below, I want you to write you own eulogy. I want you to think about your achievements, your family life, your work life and the way you lived your life. Make sure it is realistic and practical; don't imagine so hard it becomes a complete fantasy, but also, don't feel the need to be modest either.

Focus on the things you achieved in your life.

Exercise 11: Maximise Pleasure & Minimise Negative Events

During Step 1 you wrote down those things that give you pleasure and those things that make you miserable and fill you with dread. You don't need to be a psychologist to know that doing less of the latter and more of the former is going to make your life better.

Equally as important as making sure you are focusing on having more pleasurable experiences in your life it is also important to remove those that make you miserable. In the following pages list out those things that you are going to do more of and those that you are going to stop doing.

What Activities are you going to do more of?

_____

_____

_____

_____

_____

What activities are you going to do less of?

_____

_____

_____

_____

_____

Exercise 12: Personality Matching

This exercise focuses on matching your strengths with your goals and removing those things that are not authentic or focus on your weakest areas.

The next exercise after this one focuses very specifically on adapting your job as you may want to separate the two. It is up to you. You can always just complete this exercise and come back to work specific actions later if you want to.

Step 1: Re-read the summary you completed for Step 1.

Step 2: In the tables overleaf:

- Summarise your Top 6 strengths
- Summarise your Top 3 weaknesses
- Summarise your Top 3 characteristics you pretend to be

Step 3: Imagine the Actions you could do.

Take each strength and brainstorm as many actions you can undertake in your everyday life in order to use those strengths as much as possible. At this point come up with as many as you like. It often helps to talk to other people and get their ideas too.

You can write them here in your book if you have space, if not jot them down on a piece of paper as they flow into your mind.

Step 4: Pick your Favourite Actions.

Hopefully you have come up with a long list of activities for each of your 6 strengths. Realistically you won't be able to do all of them so you need to pick the most 'reasonable' for each of your key strengths. Use your intuition and judgement to identify which ones.

Write them down in the table.

Step 5: Brainstorm Actions to avoid you using weaknesses

What changes do you need to make in your life to experience less of the things you identified as the weaker aspects of your personality? The things that you aren't good at or don't enjoy.

Like you did for your strengths, brainstorm as many actions as you can think of for each and then pick your favourite actions using your own judgement and intuition.

Step 6: Write down the actions you are going undertake in the table.

Step 7: Repeat the previous steps for your non-authentic behaviours

Now complete the same brainstorming and come up with a list of actions in the table to reduce or remove non-authentic behaviours.

TOP 6 STRENGTHS

WHAT ACTIONS CAN YOU DO TO USE THESE MORE IN YOUR EVERYDAY LIFE?

TOP 3
WEAKNESSES

WHAT ACTIONS CAN YOU DO
TO USE THESE LESS IN YOUR
EVERYDAY LIFE?

TOP 3 PRETENDS YOU WANT TO REMOVE

WHAT ACTIONS DO YOU NEED TO TAKE TO PRETEND LESS IN YOUR EVERYDAY LIFE?

Exercise 13: Adapting to your Job

You may be mulling over the idea that you want to change your career and pursue another avenue that suits your personality more. However, equally, either because of financial constraints of lack of opportunity you may not be able to do that or in fact want to.

In which case you may want to make changes to your job based on what you have learnt about yourself over the last few weeks. The good news is that now you understand yourself better you can do more of what is good for you and less of what makes you miserable and does not play to your strengths.

Personally, I try to find actions where I can use my communication and people skills as much as possible. For example, I like to volunteer for speaking engagements, graduate recruitment programmes and industry conferences. Whilst I try to mix up my timetable and projects to ensure I am not doing the same things every day.

Use the tables below to map the information you have found out about yourself to our job and the activities that you undertake.

Step 1: Fill in the boxes

Write your strengths, weaknesses and non-authentic behaviours in the tables as they relate to work specifically.

Step 2: Identify where you use them today

For each strength, weakness or non-authentic behaviour write down an example of where you do experience it today at work. Spend time thinking through how and when you use them.

Step 3: Brainstorm Actions

For each of the 3 categories identify actions you can do at work in order to use more of your strengths, less of your weak areas and to stop non-authentic behaviours.

Step 4: Review with someone else

It is really useful to do this exercise with someone you work with on a regular basis or your buddy or coach. We do not always see ourselves 100% accurately and sometimes other people can provide us with great clarity.

6 KEY STRENGTHS	EXAMPLES OF USING IT AT WORK	ACTIONS TO DO MORE

3 KEY WEAKNESSES	EXAMPLES OF USING IT AT WORK	ACTIONS TO DO LESS

3 KEY NON-AUTHENTIC BEHAVIOURS	EXAMPLES OF USING IT AT WORK	ACTIONS TO STOP THESE

Exercise 14: What are you going to do for other people?

The third part of being happy and fulfilled in life is to do things for other people. In Step 1 of Kencho you thanked someone and you also did things for 3 other people in your life.

Step 1: Read back how you felt about those exercises and what you got from them.

Step 2: Read your 6 key personality strengths.

Step 3: Answer this question:

What can you realistically do in your life for other people on a regular basis that plays to your strengths?

Here are some ideas:

- Deliver collection envelopes for a charity
- Organise a local art exhibition
- Work in a charity shop free of charge for a few hours
- Volunteer to give a career's talk at the local school
- Do something about the physical appearance of your community or neighbourhood
- Put on a local play
- Paint an elderly person's house
- School reading in a deprived part of town
- Neighbourhood watch
- Run a dinner club for the elderly
- Give someone a lift to work

- Do the laundry for your partner
- Take your partner on a date once a week
- Teach people to drive
- Run a kids social club
- Set up a hobby club for like-minded people
- Give free consultancy to a charity
- Take an elderly person to the shops
- Undertake history walks for locals and tourists
- Organise a prize giving for local good citizens
- Organise a local sporting event for adults and children
- Create a local youth council
- Run a sports team for kids
- Get sponsorship for running a half marathon or walk

Step 4: Make a list of actions you would enjoy doing for other people.

Exercise 15: Prioritise your Actions

Now that you have completed the exercises in this part of your journey it is important to start to prioritise your actions. Not everything will have the same value to you and in order to ensure you are focusing on the highest value actions you need to prioritise them.

It is worth remembering that you will achieve the greatest value when the actions and activities you undertake match your personality. It is as much about how you achieve them as it is about actually realising them.

It is also worth bearing in mind that the 'value' of earning more and more money is pretty low. Money enables you to buy pleasures, but on its own it does not add to a person's sense of fulfilment or happiness. Many studies have shown that above a fairly minimal level having money doesn't add much to a person's overall sense of contentment with life.

You may be reading this and thinking that's ok for you to say, but I need to earn money to live the life I want. You will not be alone in thinking that and it is a perfectly natural thought and you should not pretend you do not have it. Just bear in mind that people who are good at what they do because their life (their job) is aligned to their personality tend to be successful and success brings wealth.

Having a job that is a good personality match brings fulfilment, fulfilment brings success and success brings money. My advice is to start at the beginning and not the end; i.e. start with personality matching, not what makes you the most money.

Step 1: List your Actions

Read back over all of the actions you identified in this steps of the journey and list them in the tables below. At this stage do not limit the number of actions you have. Write down everything that comes to mind.

YOUR ACTIONS SUMMARISED   PRIORITY

Actions for more pleasure

_____   _____

_____   _____

_____   _____

_____   _____

_____   _____

Actions for avoiding being miserable

_____   _____

_____   _____

_____   _____

_____   _____

YOUR ACTIONS SUMMARISED   PRIORITY

**Actions to achieve using more of your
personality strengths**

_____   _____

_____   _____

_____   _____

_____   _____

_____   _____

**Actions to stop pretending and move to being
yourself**

_____   _____

_____   _____

_____   _____

_____   _____

_____   _____

YOUR ACTIONS SUMMARISED   PRIORITY

**Actions to reduce or minimise behaviours that
focus on your weaknesses**

_____   _____

_____   _____

_____   _____

_____   _____

_____   _____

Actions to help other people

_____   _____

_____   _____

_____   _____

_____   _____

_____   _____

Step 2: Prioritise

Once you have listed all of the actions I want you to think about their relative importance to you. Which ones are the most important to you to start undertaking sooner rather than later. Some might give you great happiness or they might be easy to achieve. Spend time thinking of the actions and start to rank them in order; number 1 being the highest priority.

It is often best to start this exercise at both ends and work towards the middle of the list; i.e. start with the highest and the lowest priorities and work towards the middle. The ones here, in the middle, are usually the most difficult. When you feel there is not much between them just start assigning a priority based on your immediate intuition. If you don't, you may find yourself spending hours on something that is not actually that important.

STEP 3: PLAN YOUR FUTURE

Purpose: To ensure you have a clear Deliverable plan with a list of actions to undertake.
Duration: A day or so

The most successful people are not the ones with the highest IQ, but those with self-control, self-awareness, resilience and commitment with a medium to high level of intelligence. It is important to keep this in mind because the final two steps of Kencho are about addressing some of these and giving you the best chance of success.

> The definition of insanity: doing the same things over and over again, and expecting a different result.

We can be highly motivated to change, but if we keep doing the same things, running the same inappropriate patterns, our lives are not going to change, all we will experience is more and more pain and frustration. You must take action.

Many people feel overwhelmed and do not know where to start when it comes to making change happen. There seems to be so much to do and so many ideas that it is hard to know how to make it happen.

> Goals are achieved by completing Actions.

Successful people break down their actions into manageable chunks and clearly identify the actions they need to complete and by what time, in order to achieve their goals.

This is exactly what you have done over the last few pages: you now have a clear set of actions that are prioritised in terms of value to you.

Exercise 16: Twenty10 - 10 Actions in Twenty Days

One of the most effective ways to achieve your goals is to set yourself mini 20 day action plans. Twenty days is long enough to stay committed, but long enough to see or experience the results you seek. It is a great way to breakdown your overall list of actions into an achievable plan.

Make sure you have a good combination of actions that leads to more pleasure for you, better personality matching and something for other people.

Step 1: Define your first 20 Days and top 10 Actions

Look at the list of actions you identified and prioritised and think through how many you could start and, if possible, complete in the next 20 days. Make sure that at least half of them can be completed in the 20 days and not just started.

Bear in mind that 20 days is not actually that long, so choose a few high priority actions that you know you can honestly complete in the time. Most people try to do too many when they first start. Ambition is great, but some people try to do too many, fail to make many of them happen and end up feeling low. So make sure you pick 10 actions that you know you can achieve.

Do not worry about the other actions just yet, you will come back to those in the next 'Twenty10'.

Step 2: Pin it up on the Fridge

Once you have written out your Twenty10 plan make a copy and stick it to your fridge door so that you will see it every time you go to it.

TWENTY 10

Action   Date:

_____	☐
_____	☐
_____	☐
_____	☐
_____	☐
_____	☐
_____	☐
_____	☐
_____	☐
_____	☐
_____	☐
_____	☐
_____	☐
_____	☐

STEP 4: GET ON WITH IT!

C ompleting 10 actions in 20 days is how you are going to realise change and achieve a greater level of happiness and fulfilment. Once you have completed one, you are going to review what you achieved and define the next one. It is self-fuelling and once you start gaining momentum it will drive you ever forward.

You have come a long way on your transformational journey; a long way that has probably been quite emotional and sometimes surprising. Most people are surprised by some of the things they discover about themselves and their lives.

> The more I practice the luckier I get.

Hopefully, you are feeling pretty upbeat about your future and the actions you are going to take. You have a better understanding of yourself, clarity about the actions you are going to take and an initial 'Twenty10' plan to realise the highest priorities.

Some people have complete clarity at this point and start to take actions and implement changes immediately with confidence and purpose. Others get a little more nervous and start to undertake behaviours that avoid taking action.

Sometimes, and I have seen this in organisations and in individuals, people start to go over the details of the previous steps. Primarily they go over their actions again to make sure they are right or they question the validity of the plan they have created. Bottom line is that their action plan is good enough. Making it a few percent-age points better isn't going to improve the outcome; it's just going to delay them implementing changes.

There is a real risk that if you don't start taking action all of your work to date will have been a purely academic exercise. To address this, in this final step of your journey you can undertake all of the exercises at the same time. There is no need to complete them in any kind of order. At the heart are your Twenty10 plans.

Fight or Flight?

Remember we talked about fight or flight right at the beginning of this book and I asked you to think about your natural response. If you want to make positive and progressive changes to your life then you have to fight for it. You need to take immediate action, stop procrastinating and take some risks.

You have done the hard work in the previous steps of Kencho now you have to take a deep breath and get on with it. There are some other tips and actions to help you do that, but fundamentally only you can make the changes happen.

Exercise 17: Visualise Yourself Doing the Actions

I want you to do this every day until you have made the changes you want.

Step 1: Read the actions on your Twenty10 plan.

Step 2: Visualise yourself undertaking the actions you have listed in the exercise during

Step 3. Make sure you imagine how you feel undertaking the actions and how you will feel when you achieve the goals you have set yourself.

Do this every day. You can do it on the way to work, in your lunch hour, at your desk. It shouldn't take more than a few minutes.

Exercise 18: Tweet or Facebook your progress

Using social media to commit publicly is a great way to help you stay focused on your action plan. If you have been using Tweeter and Facebook during the earlier steps of Kencho then carry on; setting out your goals and keeping people up to date with progress.

If you have not been using it to date, then now is a great time to start. Tell the world what you are planning to do in the next 20 days and keep them updated. Commit publicly and you are much more likely to follow through and implement your actions.

Exercise 19: Ask Someone to Monitor your Progress

Committing to ourselves is one thing, but committing to someone else is another matter entirely. Research has found that we are much more likely to succeed in implementing changes to plan if we are monitored. It is common sense if you think about it; we do it at school, at work, with the Government, etc. We continuously hold ourselves and others accountable for plans and progress through monitoring.

Committing to your plan with another person and then meeting or talking to them on a regular basis to track progress will benefit you. The driving force is different for different personality types; some people feel obliged to complete actions, some feel guilty, others competitive, and some feel a desire to please; whatever the motivation, the output is the important thing. A change implemented, an action undertaken and ultimately a goal achieved.

It is best to meet with or speak with the person you commit to on the phone or Skype at least once a week. Be prepared to share with your action plan and the progress you have made. Do not fall in to the trap of being overly positive; keep to the facts.

If you have used a buddy or a coach through your Kencho journey then you can continue to use this person as your on-going monitor.

The one thing you need to do is keep a record of the meetings you have in your journal. How did you feel at the time? What did you achieve in that period? What challenges did you have? Do you need to change your plan?

Exercise 20: Keep a Diary

I'm not talking about keeping a daily diary of all of the things that happened to you, but keep a record of how you felt during key times and what changes and experiences you had on your journey once you started to take action.

Over the final pages of this book, write down the key things that happen to you. Write short notes that you can come back to and reflect on. You will change over the coming months and having something to look back on and reflect will allow you to see just how far you have travelled.

Exercise 21: Review your Twenty10

Step 1: At the end of each Twenty10 you need to reflect on it:

- What went well?

- What went badly?

- Did you have too many or too few actions to undertake during the 20 days?

- What did you achieve?

- Did you complete as many as you could of?

- What stopped you doing more?

Use the Notes section at the end of your book to write some notes after each Twenty10.

Step 2: Review your next set of prioritised actions

When you consider your reflections of a Twenty10 do you need to change anything for the next one to make it more successful?

Step 3: Write down the actions of your next Twenty10

As you did for the original Twenty10 write down the actions that you are going to achieve in the 20 days. Each time you do this, you will get better at judging the right actions.

Changes and Transformation are different for everyone depending on their personality and their circumstances. Sometimes small changes create large transformations, whilst at other times significant actions and energy only create small impacts.

The point is to make forward progress; to keep pushing; keep taking action and to keep challenging yourself. Inevitably your transformational journey will be different from your plan. Some of it will match, but something will come along that will have an impact and send you off into a new direction.

When it does, read back through your Kencho book, sleep on things and then realign your actions. You can adjust and add to the things you have written here as you go. It will give you a real sense of where you were and how far you have come.

OTHER INTERVENTIONS

As well as executing your actions in your plan you can also make other interventions in your life in order to make change happen and to increase the likelihood of success. I have listed out a number of interventions that will help your transformational process.

Re-read your Journey when things get tough

Looking back and reading your thoughts and the outputs of the exercises is a hugely powerful thing. It may not seem it now, if you have not already completed the book, but take my word for it. In those moments of loss of confidence or unhappiness, read back though the things you wrote and it will immediately pick you up and re-energise you.

Do Something for your Community

Hopefully during the previous steps you have identified goals and actions that you are going to undertake to help other people. Your happiness and fulfilment will be really enhanced if you do this. If the actions you undertake are aligned with your personality characteristics the sense of fulfilment will be deep and long lasting.

You need not stop there though. You can further help your own transformational change through undertaking activities for your community. This will do two things for you. One, it will enhance your own sense of fulfilment even further and two; it will inevitably make you more social. Mother Nature designed us to be social animals and the interaction and feedback you get from being part of a community and taking part in activities will enhance your life.

Aspire to be someone you admire

You have set your goals, identified your actions and laid out your plan and hopefully you are now taking action. One trick that you can use to help you even further is to identify someone you admire who already exhibits the behaviours you seek or has achieved the goals you have identified. Study that person, write down what it is about them that they do and think about how you can change and act to be more like them. What did they do to achieve their goals? What can you learn from what they did to achieve yours?

Ask Someone for Help

Asking for help is not a sign of weakness. In fact asking for help can be very liberating. If you are finding achieving your actions and goals hard work and need a little help, then ask for it. People are very glad to support each other.

Asking for and receiving help can be liberating and also inspirational to our own development and insight.

Do not dwell on the past - focus on the present and the future

One of the principles of Kencho is that dwelling on the past does not help us with the future. We live in the here and now and you have spent many weeks thinking through the future you want to create and the have put together a clear plan of how you are going to get there.

It is important that you focus on moving forward and do not get caught up dwelling on past mistakes. If during the process of Kencho you find you make mistakes or need to make changes to your goals or plan that is fine. In fact, I can guarantee that you will need to make some changes along the way.

Practice new Behaviours

Learning new behaviours and skills, as opposed to changing your personality characteristics, is probably part of your action plan. In order to make them part of your everyday life you need to practice them until they become embedded and part of you.

Distract Yourself

If you find yourself repeating behaviours that you want to change then distract yourself with something else. Do you want to stop drinking beer every night after work? Then perhaps take up running or go to the gym on the way home. Interrupt the pattern you are repeating and eventually you will stop thinking about it.

Get a Dog

If your lifestyle can accommodate it there is nothing better than getting a dog. It can help reduce stress, lower your blood pressure, distract your mind from worry, relive loneliness and give you a purpose and focus.

Focus on your Exercise and Diet

You get the idea with this one; I'm not going to preach about the benefits of exercise or a balanced diet. Suffice it to say, exercise releases chemicals that make you feel good, being fit makes you feel good about yourself and avoiding processed foods makes you less lethargic and enables you to have more energy.

Plan to Laugh

This may seem like a random exercise, but laughing is proven to make you healthier; it improves your immune system. When you are making your plans you must factor in as much opportunity for laughter that you can that matches your personality. Hopefully by this point in the process you have a good understanding of yourself and can brainstorm the activities that will enable you to laugh. Examples of the sort of things you might want to include are:

- Going to the cinema as often as possible to see a comedy
- Getting out a DVD once a week or downloading a comedy
- Watching all of those classic films you bought on VHS or DVD
- Watch re-runs or You Tube versions of your favourite TV comedy programmes
- Reading
- Going out to dinner with friends
- Buying a joke book and telling jokes
- Going to a comedy night
- Going to see comedy show

If you decide to go to a public place, like a comedy club or cinema, you will also pick up more positive vibes from sharing the experience with other people. It is worth planning to do at least some of this. List out the actions you are going to take and add them to your plan.

Pass it on

One of the best ways to do something for someone else is to help them to go through Kencho. If you have found that it has helped you change your life, become happier, more fulfilled or get stuff done then why not be a buddy for someone else.

As well as helping them you will also tap into your level 3 happiness; doing something for someone else. It is a win-win situation.

Stay Social

I mentioned right back at the beginning of this book that it can be a good idea to set up a Kencho Club. As social animals we have a natural tendency to work well in small communities and groups, especially if those groups have a similar goal and are filled with like-minded people. Think how successful Weight-Watchers, the Women's Institute and Alcoholics Anonymous are.

If you have not already done so you still can set up a club. You don't have to be too formal about it; it can take place in someone's house, in the pub, in a restaurant on Saturday morning for coffee. It is entirely up to you. The important thing is that you are talking and discussing issues, challenges, success stories and your progress with other like-minded people. After each meeting make some notes here in your journal so you can keep track of your thoughts, feelings and progress.

Do not give up. Keep taking action to change your life. Email or Tweet me and let me know what you have achieved:

✉ simon@kencho.org
🐦 @kencho345

Good luck!